SUCCESSFUL LEADERSHIP PRINCIPLES

COMMONSENSE ADVICE FOR EVERY STAGE OF YOUR CAREER

Stacey R. James

DEDICATION

To B:

Hopefully I've installed a commonsense approach to life that you will use in whatever career you embark upon. Embrace your journey, Bethany!

I love you,
~ Mama~

ଈ

FORWARD

Your life should be a story you are excited to tell.
— Adam Braun, Pencils of Promise

Born and bred in a small, rural town in the 1970's, I thought only two professional occupations existed for females: teaching and nursing. I also did not wish to become a childrearing specialist (a.k.a., a stay-at-home mom), and I could not pass for one of those God-painted beauties who graced magazine covers. I could not cut hair, and there were no waitressing jobs in the one-stoplight-town of Rustburg.

So, I honed in on teaching. Since I was relatively authoritative and organized, I figured this was the best route I could take. (Surely if my Raggedy Ann and Cheetah Monkey could get straight A's by my direction, real kids could, too!)

I quickly learned that I lacked patience. After four grueling years of college, I crashed and burned. My passion for school waned, and the chalkboard turned into green kryptonite. I did not wish to be a teacher. I just wanted a job - any job - to pay the bills. So I signed up for every on-campus interview available.

In my bright-red, $19.99 dress, sporting gold buttons and shoulder pads, I answered every question Mr. Booker asked.

"Where are you from?"

"Southern Virginia, Sir."

He asked me about my college accolades, my goals, my strengths. He told me about his team and the fun that they had. It was as if we were acquaintances, getting to know one another better. He made me feel very comfortable.

Then he asked, "Do you have any questions for me?"

I inquired, "So where do you do all of your dirty work?"

I had not researched the company and went on the assumption that because they showed compact discs on their brochure, they manufactured them. I was grossly mistaken.

I don't recall what Mr. Booker said, but I had three things going for me that day (he later told me):

- I had a technical degree (physics),
- I could communicate smartly in a thick southern accent, and
- I had a contagious smile.

Mr. Booker liked my personality, and he knew I'd fit in with the other cheap-labored grads. Unfortunately, he did not hire me on the spot.

Weeks went by. I called Miss Jordan, the Human Resources Representative. It was the first of *nine* – yes, *NINE* - calls I'd make to her, following up on my status. I wanted a job - THAT job - because it felt right. I was ruthless in my pursuit. My best friend was moving to

Northern Virginia to be a business woman and I wanted to be one, too! Time to leave my little one-horse town.

My family was none too happy that I intended on venturing into a world four hours away, but it was time to spread my wings – and that I did.

Don't let your small beginnings make you small minded.
— **Brendon Burchard**

❧

I'm so glad that early in my career, women developed choices like never before. Many powerful women leaped out of my television and into my conscious – from Wonder Woman and Charlie's Angel's, to Anita Hill and Sandra Day O'Connor. Today the amount of women participating in the formerly man's world is astounding. There are women soldiers, electricians, and even possibly president!

Often, people from my hometown have asked me what I did for a living. "In layman's terms," I replied, " I manage a bunch of really old men."

It's true. Many of my teams in my government-contracting career have consisted of retired military men. Men more than double my age. Although they were experts in their field, they needed someone like me to help them stay on task. I had to learn military-speak ("Alpha," "Bravo," Charlie"), and their ranks and rates. I had to figure out how various systems onboard a vessel operated, who built them, and how they were maintained. (This was quite an achievement for a young woman who had never set foot upon any craft larger than a John Boat on a rural pond!)

The subject matter didn't matter. My ability to stay organized and rule with a smile allowed me to excel at my job. I discovered I possessed drive, determination, and the ability to encourage others to do what I needed them to do. I also listened and learned from my subordinates. Mastering all of these traits I became a successful leader.

Leadership is innate to many, but sadly, it is lacking in today's world. Hard-to-understand doctrine and ideals have overshadowed simple truths for way too long. True leadership cannot be taught. A degree does not guarantee it.

This collection of commonsense principles is based on my own observations and experiences. I would be remiss if I did not mention my folks. They were the impetus to the commonsense roots of this book. Dad, a stroke victim, exhibited determination, stubbornness, and a zeal for life; Mama proved to me that women could do anything a man could do; and Nannie, taught me that "hard work never killed anyone."

The book is organized into three parts: for those who are just embarking upon their career, to a mid-level professional, and finally a seasoned veteran. It assumes the reader works in an office environment, but it can apply to anyone in a leadership role - whether you are a coach, small business owner, or president of a major corporation. (Heck, if I shifted a few paragraphs and changed some verbiage, this book could be a self-help magnum opus!)

There are quotes scattered throughout this book that I have collected over the years from successful entrepreneurs, celebrities, historical figures, and writers. I hope these tidbits help you and your teams achieve much success!

Best of luck in all your endeavors!

MAKINGS OF A LEADER

BUILDING A SUCCESSFUL FOUNDATION

After college, my two girlfriends and I moved into a two bedroom apartment. Three girls sharing two bedrooms. It was as if we had never left college! But it was all we could afford. I even washed my sandwich bags to save money!

Since I could not afford the $200/month parking at my office, I had to take the metro. Each day, I walked to the Merrifield metro, hopped aboard, and looked around at the dreary faces, peering into their newspapers. I did not like this at all. My soul did not like it, and my feet did not like it. I wore out multiple pairs of Payless pumps, walking to and from the underground metro.

Always looking for better, I joined a carpool. More cheerful than the metro, however, it consisted of very poor drivers. Five of us squeezed into my Aqua Blue Dodge Shadow for a week at a time once per month. My car outranked Doug's red-wagon Pinto because his was dirty, and he had a dashboard-mounted antenna that I knew would stab me if ever he slammed on the brakes too hard.

At my job, my smile awarded me a raise, for the wicked witch customer preferred my services over that of my peers. Lucky me! She tried my patience, but my patience won out. I'd deliver a document to her ten blocks away, only to have her reject it. I walked back to my office, made the necessary changes and walked it back to her within the hour. Heel blisters popped, as did the nails from my shoe's heels, but I always delivered, exceeding her expectations. I won her heart, her friendship, and she instigated my promotion!

1. Love yourself

There is a reason that I am going to begin and end this book with this main concept. Do not let outside influences impact your love of self. You are worthy!

In order for others to love you, you must love yourself. Take a vow right now to be true to yourself. Be proud of your accomplishments throughout each stage of your life. Don't have any regrets. Honor this one life that has been given to you. Trust me, as you get older, the days go by more quickly!

Part of loving yourself is knowing yourself. Since I had tossed myself into city-life and government work, I missed the interaction between customers that I had once had in high school when I worked at a bookstore. I could not quit my day-job, for I was now an adult and had to pay rent, my car payment and food that was more substantial than Ramen Noodles. So I sought out a second job to quench the hunger of my soul. (Not many people know this about me, but that second job was at a candy store!)

Knowing what your soul lacks and taking action is the crux of loving yourself.

The future belongs to those who believe in the beauty of their dreams.
— Eleanor Roosevelt

ᘓ♥

2. Be who you want to be

Remember when you pretended to be a superhero as a child? Chances are, you had the enthusiasm and mind-frame to conquer the world! Why give this up when you grow up?

You are a blank canvas. Don't let anyone else paint on it. Only you should determine who you are and who you want to be. Act the part and become that person.

Your purpose in life is to find your purpose and give your whole heart and soul to it.

- Buddha

&❧

3. Tryout different jobs

One of my biggest mistakes was not trying out other opportunities prior to starting my career.

It is difficult to get out of a career field once you enter it. Volunteer, shadow, work part-time. You owe it to yourself to do whatever it is you feel passionate about. Once you acquire a family and mortgage, it is difficult to find money or the time to pursue another route.

Figure it out in the pond.

— Ina Garten

&❧

4. Get to know the gatekeeper

Receptionists, assistants, and secretaries are gatekeepers to the big boss. Getting to know the gatekeeper can work to your advantage. They know more than their title infers. They are usually very powerful because they know the boss' schedule and even what drives him or her.

Do your homework. Make yourself visible by asking pertinent questions that leave them spellbound. Knowing small tidbits about the boss that your competition does now will help you break the ice. You will be remembered.

Never take no from a person who has no authority to say yes.
— Adam Braun, *Pencils of Promise*

&

5. About interviewing

Interviewing should not be scary or difficult. All you need to do is prepare.

Study your resume and think of all your accomplishments. What are you most proud of? What are your biggest strengths? Be prepared to tell real-life stories that support your accomplishments. An interview should be 3-dimensional, not 2-dimensional.

The interviewer is a person just like you. They want to know that a candidate is competent and enthusiastic.

Be yourself.

Also, study the company. Look on their website and learn everything you can about what they do. Read news articles about the company and its industry.

Don't leave an interview without asking questions. Here are three questions you should ask so that you understand if you made the cut prior to walking out the door:

- "How long have you been interviewing for this position?"
- "What have you not found in other candidates that you would like to find?"
- "How does what I have to offer stack up against what you need?"

Remember, you are interviewing them just as much as they are interviewing you. Sell yourself, but don't settle.

You may be rejected after an interview. Who cares? It isn't the end of the world. Remember J.K. Rowling? Author of the Harry Potter book series? She received rejection letter after rejection letter when she tried to publish the now world-famous book. She did not give up! Lesson learned: Don't let one bad interview or rejection notice get you down!

6. Read the fine print

It is important to fully read an offer letter before accepting a job, especially any Non-Disclosure Agreements (NDAs).

I made this mistake fairly early in my career. My first boss called me into his office one morning. He, his boss, and three others on the leadership team told me that they were leaving the company the next day. They presented me with an offer letter, told me I had one night to think about it, and I could not tell anyone.

About twenty peons like myself, trusting our leaders and wanting more money, left with them.

The very first day at the new company, an injunction was placed upon us because we had signed an NDA upon accepting employment with the initial company. I was so happy to get a job, I had not paid attention to what I signed. Clearly, I should have.

For nearly six months, I twiddled my thumbs while the two companies fought. Finally, I accepted a lateral transfer into another department, breaking away from those old bosses and teammates.

I now read every detail of employment paperwork. It is essential to accepting future employment offers.

7. Dress Appropriately

Appearance matters, like it or not.

Gone are the days of wearing a boring, black suits. Wear what you wish, but make sure you are clean, professional, and well-groomed - both before and after you get the job.

Do not look sloppy. Be neat and approachable. Wear deodorant. Don't wear too much perfume, and don't show any cleavage. (As a manager, you don't know how many times I've had to find creative ways to tell an employee that he stinks, or that a women employee needed to hide "the girls.")

There are many books and magazine articles dedicated to dress so there is no need for me to expand on what to wear. Stay up-to-date on current styles. Stay classy.

Remember that even if those around you dress down, it is best to dress slightly better than them. Look the part you want to play.

Shoes are important, too. Did you know that people can be defined by their shoes?

Firstly, make sure your shoes are not outdated. Make sure they fit well. If you have never worn heels, don't start by wearing them to an interview. Chances are, your heavy step will make you look clunky or shaky.

Coordinate shoes with your belt (guys) and your purse (girls). Buff out any scuff marks. Literally, you should, "Put your best foot forward."

8. Leave a clean desk at the end of every day

Aside from a happy demeanor, and a nice appearance, you also need to be able to "live" with those around you. At work, you spend 6-10 hours a day with people of all backgrounds. Don't be a pig-pen. Organize your space. Keep your work area neat.

You cannot leave a mess on your desk or workstation and expect to hit the ground running when you arrive the next morning. File away papers, put away tools, update your to-do list and be ready. You will be able to leave work happily, knowing you will be ready to tackle anything the next day.

9. Personalize your space

Ever marveled at the corner office's décor? Rich leathers, diplomas in view touting accomplishments, and small pictures of happy families, dogs and well-known monuments? Executives do it – why shouldn't you?

You may not have much room in your cubicle, but if you are there for 8 hours, make your space your own.

However, don't go overboard. Don't bring in all your yard sale finds, making coworkers nominate you for the television show about hoarders. Instead, drink out of your favorite coffee mug; showcase nicely-framed pictures of loved ones; tout your diploma; use a customized mouse and mousepad; cushion your chair with a small, decorative pillow; dedicate one drawer to healthy snacks; stock colorful sticky notes, fancy pens that write perfectly; add a small basket to hold trinkets and hand lotion. If you are an avid football fan, hang a small pennant. You get the idea. Show that you're a person, not a robot, and you will be respected as such.

10. Organize shared files

Think about your work product. How should you organize your files so you can remain on top of your game? Perhaps you need to load all of your files onto a phone or a laptop if you are mobile. Maybe you need a contact list with addresses so you can visit clients at a moment's notice. Perhaps you need colored folders when filing. Staples may be better than paperclips, or maybe you don't use paper at all. Organizational styles vary from person to person, job to job.

Maintain electronic records vice hard-copies if at all possible. The environment will thank you, and you're less prone to paper cuts.

Electronic files can become as cluttered as file cabinets. Prevent server overload by retaining only one copy of email threads. Regularly clean and organize your desktop on your computer. Some desktops can become as cluttered as your work area.

Whatever your organizational style, be certain it is as efficient as possible. Do not expect others to follow your style. If you must share files with others, agree on a format and a procedure.

11. Make lists

I love making lists! It gives me great pleasure to start a fresh list and be able to check things off as I complete them. I have all types of lists: grocery lists, chore lists, gear lists for running, vacation packing lists, etc. I would not have accomplished nearly as much in my lifetime had I not used lists!

I particularly like index cards. I keep a stash in my car, beside the television remote, on my desk and beside my bed. Index cards are sturdy enough to not be destroyed and cheap enough to toss after I've completed everything on my list each day. I also have a journal in which I keep any long-term lists. For example, in my journal I keep my "Christmas Presents to Buy" list as well as my list of career goals.

12. Email details

Have you ever been scolded in an email? Have you written an email, only to have it taken the wrong way by the recipient? How effectively do you get your tone across in an email? Typing, like the tongue, can cause you to fall by the edge of the sword. Tread carefully!

Let's face it – not all of us were English Majors, and not all of us are eloquent speakers. How do you ensure you are getting your point across, both with the facts and the underlying meaning, emotion, or connotations?

One way is by injecting punctuation and emoticons, just as you would a text message. For example, here are three ways of saying the exact same thing:

1. *Your concern over the issue is not going over well with me AT ALL.*
2. *Your concern is not valid.*
3. *Your concern, although not exactly valid, is totally understandable!!! ☺*

Which one would you rather receive? The punctuation and emoticons help to further the intent of the author. Being too direct, without emotion either way, is open for interpretation and could be detrimental to your intent.

Be creative with email subject lines. Let the recipient know what action he/she needs to take with the email. You don't have to write a book each time as long as your intent is stated up front. What you type in the subject line sets the tone for the email. Be specific. For example:

Subject: For Your Records: Closeout Report, Task 10-007

Do not place any verbiage within the email, only your signature and contact information. This tells the reader to read and file the attached report. No action is required by the reader.

Another example is:
For Your Review/Approval: Draft Marketing Report on the Banks Account

This tells the reader she needs to take action.

Another inference that can be made by a recipient is why someone was copied on an e-mail. Why was Mr. Banks copied on the e-mail? He's the next manager up on the chain. Did I do something wrong? Did my boss do this because he wanted to or because he had to?

Feelings can snowball here, too. Also, does Mr. Banks

even know why he is being copied on the e-mail?

To be safe, explain why you are copying someone. This helps all parties understand your reasons. In this particular case, the author should have said,

"David, I am copying Mr. Banks on this email because I want him to understand your concerns, too, so that he can decide whether or not they should be raised at the next corporate meeting."

Maybe you don't have time to do this each time, but it will only help you be an effective communicator. Truly think about what your intent is each time and try to understand the perceptions of each recipient.

Email signatures should include your name, position, company, and contact information. They should not contain quotes. (Save your quotes for Facebook.)

If anyone tries to condemn you in an email, you have two choices: ignore them, or state the facts and move on. I prefer the latter of the two because you have your reputation to uphold.

For example, if a client swears you did not deliver a document by the due date, find your email where you discussed changing the due date and forward it to him and anyone else he or she had copied on their e-mail. Yes, you are calling out their mistake, but you are showing your worth and that you are not one to be reckoned with. If you did let the due date slip by, apologize for the mistake, send them the deliverable, and move on. No need to wallow in shame or defend yourself with multiple excuses.

Remember not only to say the right thing in the right place, but far more difficult still, to leave unsaid the wrong thing at the tempting moment.
- Benjamin Franklin

&♭

13. Book all meetings through an electronic calendar

Using an electronic calendar system like that in Microsoft Outlook enables your coworkers to see your schedule. This advises them of when they should schedule meetings if they want you to attend.

You can change your settings to alert you 15 minutes prior to the start of a meeting. This gives you time to complete what you are doing and make any last minute preparations.

14. Get noticed, yet remain humble

We all know an office "Bragasaurus" - someone who constantly brags of his or her accomplishments. Don't become one. This ostentatious employee irritates others because they have difficulty relishing in anyone else's successes. Check your ego at the door.

How do you get noticed without being a jerk?
- Honk your own horn in a humble way.
- Bubble from the inside out.
- Be yourself.
- Be direct, yet pleasant, not loud or annoying.
- Be persistent.
- Develop an elevator sales pitch. Market yourself in 60-seconds or less to each new person you meet.

Use creativity to get noticed. Send a small cake to a recruiter with a slice missing. Enclose a note with the cake, stating, "I'm your missing piece!" That gets attention!

Those employees who are well-known and well-liked outshine others because of their attitude and their aura. They aren't necessarily the smartest or brightest.

15. Become indispensable

Starting out in the workforce, you are the low man on the totem pole. Learn EVERYTHING you can, no matter how miniscule it may seem. Expect growing pains.

You will be called upon to make copies, sort, and file. You may have to clean the coffee pot each day, and run to the store to get more when the office runs out.

With the right attitude though, your hard work will pay off. You won't be the low man on the totem pole for long.

Here are some little things to make sure you know:
- how to change ink in the printer
- where to find more paper
- how to make 2-sided copies
- on what type of contract you are working
- when the company was founded
- your boss's wife's name
- your client's favorite color

The more you know, the more you will be called upon, and the more indispensable to the company you become.

Knowledge is power. As much as you gain insight by experience, you can also gain it through reading. Listen to audiobooks as you commute to work. Take time to perfect your craft.

16. Seek forgiveness later

Do not seek your boss' approval on every minor detail. They are too busy. Instead, if something is a really good idea, run it by a colleague or two. If they think it's a good idea, implement it on the spot.

Being proactive rarely hurts you. You were hired for a reason. Be professional and prove that your boss does not need to babysit you.

Mistakes are always forgivable, if one has the courage to admit them.

- Bruce Lee

᪶

17. Keep your boss out of trouble

If you want your boss to have your back, have theirs.

Your boss is a person, just like you. They're not perfect. They have families, hobbies, and face illnesses and losses. They deal with flat tires, sick children, and occasional hangovers.

No matter how much you disagree with your boss, do not bypass them and go to their manager. Unless someone is in danger, give your boss the benefit-of-the-doubt in answering questions or concerns. Be tactful and honest. They will appreciate and respect you in the long run. Remember, your immediate boss is usually the one conducting your review.

You may disagree with your boss, but never discredit him or her. Look at the positives and what got them into their position. Chances are you can learn from them. No one is perfect. Neither are you.

Because telecommuting is commonplace, your boss may work at a corporate office over five hours away. There has to be trust, so make sure you do not give him or her a reason to mistrust you. Your boss should be able to trust you emphatically. Be grateful of a boss who does not micromanage you. Communicate just enough without being a nuisance.

Sing your boss's praises to upper management whenever you get a chance.

Never try to "up one" on your boss. Don't skip the chain-of-command. Respect for this person can make (or break) your career.

Sometimes they dig their own graves, but don't give them the shovel!

18. Accept constructive criticism

Business is business. Do not take criticism personally.

You will make mistakes along the way. Be accountable for your actions. Accept responsibility. Don't make excuses, or blame others. Do not complain when you don't get what you want. A killjoy attitude gets you nowhere.

If you must cry, go to the bathroom stall until you've regained your composure. The business world is not for the tender-hearted. Toughen up!

Do your best, and be honest with your manager and peers. Do not be afraid to ask for feedback just because you think it is going to be critical. Expand your perspective by listening to that of others.

My Dad always said, "Practice, practice, practice!" Even the most professional football players practice often to perfect their game. Accept criticism from a boss as you would a coach on a football field. You are *practicing*. And practicing leads to improvements, no matter how small.

19. Tell it like it is

Upper management appreciates honesty. They want someone who will tell them the truth and not talk in circles. They want someone who will present innovative ideas, and help them see what they may be missing.

Communication is the key to success in every aspect of life. Some want their boss to think everything is perfect when it is not. Tell your boss what's wrong and how you intend on making it better, if not perfect.

Be frank and direct. Remain professional, without an attitude. Find your true voice, a voice of reason. Take out the emotion.

You can be a spitfire in the office, but not without reason. Portraying a positive attitude, even when disagreeing with someone, will earn you points in the game of life. When you speak, do so with an air of confidence, openness and honesty. Always encourage and cheer on others.

Things cannot and will not continue downward forever; they will always turn around.
　　　　　　　－ Donald Trump, *Think Big and Kick Ass*

&♦

20. Take your lunch break

Many of us are guilty of eating at our desks. Don't do it. Not only will you probably eat more without even realizing it, but it looks unprofessional. Plus, you need a break!

Don't assume your boss will penalize you for taking your law-given break. Even if you are not hungry, run errands, or bring your exercise gear and go for a walk outside. Taking a midday break prevents burnout.

21. Get enough sleep

Throughout the stages of life, there will be times that you lack sleep. You may be awake in the middle of the night, coaxing a small child back to bed. You may need to take a potty-training puppy outside for a brief walk. Or, you may be in the bathroom, thinking you should have stopped at two glasses of wine earlier that evening! The lack of sleep negatively affects your performance at work. Try to get 7-8 hours of quality sleep each night so you can remain fresh the next day.

22. Be well-rounded

You may feel that being a "jack of all trades, master of none" is a hindrance to your career. I thought so, too, until a coworker told me, "You are the best type of employee out there. You are the utility player that can be put anywhere to do anything! Perfect!"

How can you build your versatility muscle? Expose yourself to restaurants, movies, and places that you wouldn't ordinarily frequent. Allow yourself to be open to new possibilities. Take chances that enable you to grow and learn. Be a sponge.

23. Don't be too hard on yourself

Sometimes, we can be our own worst critics. It is important that we do not give into negative self-talk, because we may start to believe it.

When you find yourself becoming negative, take a step back and reflect. Perhaps you are trying to do too much. Do not be afraid to ask your boss or others for help. They will respect you if you do. Don't conceal a major problem from them because more than likely, it will eventually blow up.

As I said previously, we are not robots, but human. We will make mistakes. It's okay! Learn from them, apologize if you need to, and move on. Every loss leads to a gain.

Don't try to be perfect. It is okay to aim for perfection in a deliverable or product, but sometimes you have to accept that putting forth your best effort and finishing on-time is better than spinning around in circles and being late.

Never give up, for that is just the place and time that the tide will turn.

- Harriet Beecher Stowe

&♥

24. Ask for guidance and take notes

It is impossible to know everything. You may think you know it all, but you don't. You will make mistakes, but you will make fewer if you ask questions.

When I learn something new at work, I quickly jot down notes as I receive instructions. They are usually quite messy, however I am able to decipher them enough to re-write them later when I am back at my desk. This not only reinforces what I have learned, but it enables me to ask questions about any lingering questions, and it gives me a permanent guidebook to follow in the future and for future employees.

25. Enlist mentors

Successful people surround themselves with other successful people. Ever notice how celebrities play golf together, dine in fancy restaurants, and send their children to the same schools? Success breeds success.

You may not be a celebrity, but you can surround yourself with people in your profession that have mastered it. Remember the master/apprentice relationships of yesteryear? Today, we call this type of relationship *mentoring*.

A mentor does not have to be a person you know. You may not work closely with your mentor or even be in the same city together. You don't even have to really know them. Sure, it is good to have a person with whom you can converse and ask questions, but you can also learn from the masters of your field. Read their books, and attend their lectures.

You can always find someone wiser than yourself. Their wisdom may be due to age, education, or experience. Tap into this wisdom. Don't make the same mistakes or reinvent the wheel. Use this invaluable resource. Continue to learn from those that have faced similar issues to what you may be facing. Imitate, then innovate.

It was my teacher's genius, her quick sympathy, her loving tact which made the first years of my education so beautiful.

- Helen Keller

δ♥

26. Appreciate what you have

Learn from your dog the next time you walk him. He doesn't care about where he's going. He is happy to bask in the here and now.

We are all walking towards something, hopefully in the direction of something to better our lives: fame, fortune, and love. We may want to move to a new city, find a new job, or give birth to another child. Perhaps we want a new car or a new article of clothing.

Seriously reflect on why you want these things. If exploring new thoughts and opening yourself up to new challenges fuels your flame, fine. You may not need to shake things up quite so much if you are just bored.

Boredom is usually temporary. You may only need to tweak one small thing to energize you.

Truly soul-search before making huge purchases or life-altering moves. Appreciate what you have, and appreciate the risks you take. You do not have to settle at any point in your life.

27. Know your Value

Make sure your compensation is commensurate with your duties.

How do you do this? Look at job announcements and find similar job descriptions. Websites such as Glassdoor.com and Indeed.com post salary ranges. Do not shortchange yourself. Ask for a raise if warranted. It won't happen if you don't ask. Just make sure that when you ask for a raise, you present all of the reasons you deserve one. Provide concrete data to support your request.

Know your value.

- Nika Brzezinski

&

28. Show gratitude

Always thank and compliment others. Leave your desk and visit your coworkers at their cubicles. Introduce yourself in the lunch/break room. Make small talk. Open up about yourself. Be kind and respectful in meetings and in emails.

Be grateful for what you have and stop complaining - it bores everybody else, does you no good, and doesn't solve any problems.

-Zig Ziglar

&❧

29. Ask others check your work

Performing a peer review is a great way to both assist a coworker while learning something in the process. You can provide invaluable feedback before it is presented to a client, injecting quality assurance into the collective work of the company.

You may not work on the same contract. You may even have to review the document on your own time, but the extra effort you expend could pay dividends to the company and your overall performance.

Feel honored that you have been asked to review someone's prized possession. They may have worked tirelessly on a project or document. They are giving it to you because they feel safe doing so while valuing your expert opinion. It's called trust. Maybe you are a "tell-it-like-it-is" coworker, who is genuine and kindhearted. What a compliment!

Now that you understand the value of a peer review, there are some questions you should ask before conducting it:

1. When is the project due to the client? Find out the deadline. When does your coworker need your feedback? Agree to a date/time and stick to it. Chisel time out of your schedule in the evening to give it your undivided attention. Don't skim over it while sitting at a soccer game.
2. What were the initial requirements? Get a copy of the Statement of Work (SOW) and ensure your coworker followed them.
3. What does your coworker specifically want you to pay attention to? There is a section of the project they may feel queasy about. Glean from them their suspected trouble spots.
4. Determine the audience. Voice matters. Will the customer understand everything there is to understand?

While format is important, it isn't the end-all and unfortunately it is the first – and sometimes only - thing reviewers check.

Constructive criticism is about finding something good and positive to soften the blow.
- Paula Abdul

&♦

30. Beware of Cliques

You are likely to switch jobs several times in your career. As the new kid on the block you will notice some established cliques in the organization. There's the young party crowd, the workout crew, the overachievers. It has been my experience that you do not need to be part of a clique in order to succeed. Be friendly with everyone and they, in turn, will be friendly to you!

31. Participate in Social Media

Social networking can increase your chances of expanding your network and your net worth. Sign up for the latest social media websites (LinkedIn, Facebook, Twitter, etc.) and use them to your advantage. Remember though, a good rule of thumb is: DON'T POST ANYTHING YOU WOULD NOT WANT YOUR GRANDMOTHER TO SEE!

Have a squeaky-clean profile that portrays your likeable side. Do not allow any skeletons to escape the closet.

My readers and my audiences have turned into my followers.
                                        - Jeffrey Gitomer

&

32. Deflect drama

Almost every office employs a drama queen or king. This person usually is the one who talks behind others' backs. They instigate problems that did not need to be raised in the first place. They cause panic and over-embellish issues.

Do not involve yourself in office drama, gossip, or politics. It is never a good idea. There is no reason to bring a bag full of emotions with you to work. Respect others and tactfully exit the watercooler area when topics begin heading in a negative direction.

33. Control yourself at social settings

At my very first job after college, I recall donning my green satin dress with the hot pink bow and black velvet top. I took the metro into the Army-Navy Country Club where my employer was hosting its annual holiday party. I was excited about dressing up and socializing with my coworkers outside of work!

As with every holiday party, there was a plethora of finger food, beer and wine. There was also a DJ playing "The Electric Slide."

Well, I slid alright! As I meandered to the stage with wine glass in hand to collect my door prize (a Black-and-Decker flashlight), I fell down a small flight of stairs. Green satin fell backwards over my hips, exposing my underside. Can we say, "Embarrassing?" Luckily my boss had already left the event, but my co-workers never let me forget about that incident.

It was a good lesson to learn early in my career. Let me save you from the same mistake: Limit your alcohol intake at corporate events!

34. Have a sense of humor

That last story feeds directly into this tidbit. Being able to laugh at yourself is a milestone of maturity. It keeps you humble and makes others like you!

There is nothing in the world so irresistibly contagious as laughter and good humor.
> — Charles Dickens, A Christmas Carol

৬৹

35. Conquer your Fears

You're presenting a brief in front of the harshest of clients. Your palms are sweaty, your feet, cold. You are practically paralyzed with fear. You've tried imagining him without underwear, but that is only causing you further distress.

To free yourself from insecurities visualize a positive image of the situation. Imagine feeling calm and cool, speaking eloquently to a very happy customer, who, by-the-way, is holding a pen in one hand, a checkbook in the other! Mitigate fear by only allowing yourself to visualize a positive outcome.

When you are afraid, break down your concerns into actionable components. Owning a business seems like a daunting task. You want to start your own roofing company, but you do not know where to begin. There are tax laws, building codes, certifications, etc. Your dream seems like an insurmountable wall. You never find the time to get started. If you do, at some point, you simply give up.

Instead, set aside time each day to study. Make "to do" lists. Talk to key people. Find a mentor. Learn how to compete smartly against your competitors.

You can only begin to make your dream a reality by rejecting fear and taking action.

Feel the fear and do it anyway.

- Susan Jeffers

&❧

36. Exude confidence

Be that positive person that everyone wants to befriend. Talk with everyone – the grocer, fellow neighborhood dog walkers, soccer parents, the yoga instructor. Periodically walk around the office. Visit other offices. Say hello to the street vendor. Leave your comfort zone. Host a party with all your new acquaintances. Who knows – they may become part of your extended family.

You cannot grow by remaining in a shell. When you see someone you would like to meet, realize that they are just like you. They, too, may want to make you one of their new contacts.

Control your own destiny or someone else will.

– Jack Welsh

&❧

EFFECTIVE LEADERSHIP

WHAT GOOD LEADERS DO

In a few years, I had earned the trust of upper management and was given more authority. With the encouragement of one of my supervisors, I opted to take the 4-hour Project Management Professional exam to boost my credentials. The stage was now set for me to direct a cast of employees.

Once my baby was born, I started to rethink what it meant to be a woman with a career. I read angry debates on the internet between stay-at-home mothers and working mothers about what was best for children. Together, my baby and I decided what was best for us. Because she nursed and would not drink from any bottle, I left full time employment and found a great part-time job in a similar field. It was in this position that I believe my career really excelled.

Years later, divorce caused me again to pause. Luckily I had excellent coworkers who enabled me to lean upon them and push through the pain. I stepped up to the plate and became a leader, a manager. Not only because I had to, but because it was in my nature. Again, even though I had hit another obstacle, my career sprang forth once again in a new direction.

This opportunity allowed me to travel and see our country's coasts. I learned how to test breathing apparatus and I crawled around the belly of ships. This was also the time in my life where I honed in on giving my strength a title: Project Manager Professional.

Yet another title I assumed during this period was Author. I learned that books were family, and I could give birth to my own.

37. Network

Powerful businessmen and businesswomen work their contacts.

As you grow your career, never stop networking and building friendships. You don't have to be the most outgoing individual to gain and keep contacts. Feel self-assured. You can handle whatever comes your way. Empower yourself to meet and interact with strangers.

Foster relationships to keep the lines of communication and civility open. It's the primary reason embassies and heads of states exist.

38. Attend conferences

Today, companies rarely have spare change within their budgets to fund conferences or symposiums – places where employees within a certain industry can market, collaborate and exchange innovative ideas.

The benefit of attending conferences according to Keith Ferrazzi, in his book, *Never Eat Alone*, is not for insight or education, but rather making contacts. Quality relationships lead to success.

If you are lucky enough to attend a conference, use it to your advantage. Don't be a wallflower with your head stuck in the brochure, walking from booth to booth without purpose. Do not allow it to be just a boondoggle. Don't just visit booths and pick up trinkets. Instead, get to know the companies, their representatives and their products.

If you own a small company and don't have the funds for a conference, hold a small open house. Invite key customers and stakeholders.

There really is some meaning behind the cliché, "It isn't what you know, but who you know."

39. Present briefs like a pro

If you are giving a brief, don't bore your audience. Strategize. The way you present yourself and your material can either make you a captivating speaker or a sandman. Here are some suggestions on keeping audience alive and awake:

- Use short, fragmented statements to capture a thought. More detailed information can go in the notes section of your presentation.
- Include only 5 statements per slide. Any more than that and you will begin to see closed eyes and open mouths.
- Include pertinent pictures and graphs. Unless you are in the toy business, avoid clipart and cartoons because they are considered juvenile in the business world.
- Use a simple colored background instead of white, especially if you do not have to provide copies to the attendees. White can become boring and yawn... mundane.
- Include sidebars and hyperlinks. Ensure they are not too tiny, and only add them if they enhance the information on the slide.

- Select the appropriate font and font size for the size of your venue. Arrive at the venue 30 minutes early to test the equipment and ensure the brief can be seen and deciphered from every area of the room.

As for content:
- Use present tense and action verbs.
- Eliminate filler words. Again, slides should contain only fragments.
- Include transition slides. Transition slides are those slides with only one word that introduce a topic. These are important because they capture the viewers' attention and alerts them of what's next.

And finally, the delivery:
- Speak with confidence and without a flat, monotonous voice. Entertain with purpose.
- Know your audience. If the audience consists of your peers, for example, there is no need to define acronyms.
- Refer to each line of your brief. If you have used fragments, as I suggested above, you can easily read these fragments and then go into details verbally before moving onto the next line.
- If there is no reason to walk around, don't. You may step from behind the podium only if it comes naturally to you. It can be an effective way of connecting with your audience. Pacing, however, changes the focus from the briefing to you, and you are not in a Broadway play.

- Practice your brief to ensure your slides flow. You may want to invite a coworker to listen to your run-through.

Should you be new to giving briefs, you may want to join your local Toastmasters Group. Toastmasters is an organization that helps you improve your speaking/delivery. (Visit www.toastmasters.org for additional information.)

40. Communicate

Communication is a two-way street. Oftentimes, companies relay information, but rarely do they listen to commonsense ideas their employees may have.

Frequent communication is required by companies to retain employees and maintain morale. Meanwhile, employees must communicate up the chain to improve processes.

Here are some ideas for you to improve communication if you are a manager:

1. Distribute a daily voicemail or email with an inspirational thought.
2. Periodically, select and recognize a star employee for their accomplishments in front of their peers (one of the best motivational and team building tools available).
3. Institute brown-bag lunches. These are not mandatory, but allow employees to meet on their lunch break to discuss topics of concern.

4. Distribute a monthly or quarterly newsletter with substance. Let your employees know how the company is doing.
5. Send out a survey to glean important information from your employees.

Employees who are well-informed feel they are included as part of a larger goal. They view what they do as a career, not a job. In a career, an employee is always thinking how to better themselves. In a job, they go to work, spin a wheel, return home, and then repeat it again the next day. Fortune 500 companies understand this philosophy very well.

The leader who can communicate powerfully and prolifically, build relationships, inspire and motivate others, and foster collaboration in a geographically dispersed organization, distinguishes good leaders from extraordinary leaders!

41. Hold periodic meetings

Leaders should be seen and heard often. Quality remote meetings are a necessity in dispersed organizations.

Identify your information delivery systems (Intranets, blogs, e-newsletters, video conferences, email blasts, etc.). Ensure each team member has the ability to join in using the tool of choice.

Make meetings a habit in your organization. Discuss business priorities. Table topics when questions go off on a tangent. Without a regular, mandatory meetings, dispersed employees would never gather as a team.

Keep the communication framework strong. Require in-person meetings sometimes as well. Authenticate your leadership role and reinforce your message to ensure everyone is on the same page.

Only two companies for which I have worked held regular quarterly meetings. At these events, the CEO presented statistics on the company's financial well-being, presented awards, and shared his intentions for the upcoming quarter. He was our commander, effectively unifying us, and enabling us to share in a common mission.

Think big.

— Donald Trump

&❧

42. Listen

One of the things that separates humans from animals is that we can feel empathy and think from different perspectives. Do not get so caught up in your own beliefs that you can't see someone else's point of view.

I once wrote an article for a professional magazine entitled, *Personal Touch - Smaller company conducive to more customer quality time.* It chronicled how I left a large company and went to a smaller one where not only clients benefitted from better quality service, but I reaped the benefits of being part of a "Cheers-like" family. Everyone knew my name, for I was not just another number.

A year later, after a large contract win with a government agency, I was faced with managing twenty task orders that came with 20+ employees and 20+ customers. It was extremely difficult to keep everyone happy. Meanwhile, I still was expected to meet our corporate office's every demand, "Approve your employee's timecards!" "Get these progress reports signed by tomorrow!" I was a basket case. It was taking its toll on my health.

One day, I pulled out my published article. "Wait a minute!" I exclaimed, "My Company needs to read this! There are things we can do better! There should be a cap on how many task orders our managers are expected to manage! If we do not grow smartly, and grow our infrastructure in the right manner, we will lose our competitive edge. We won't win additional contracts in the future!"

I contacted my supervisor immediately. "Joel, I hate to say I cannot do something, but I honestly cannot handle this many task orders. I'm speaking on behalf of ALL the company's frontline managers."

My patience (again, not one of my strongest virtues) was put to the test. I preached to Joel almost daily about our quality and its demise over the year. I saw it in the faces of our clients. When they looked at a report - draft or final - there were frowns. We were no longer exceeding expectations. We were barely meeting them.

Finally, with my persistence and Joel's charming attitude, we made the upper echelons of the company realize that for the sake quality they needed to listen.

They commenced scheduling meetings for their project managers. Half of my tasks were scraped from my overloaded plate. They purchased a more robust accounting system, and developed a much-needed organizational chart.

The general rule of thumb is to listen 80% and talk 20%.

43. Earn your team's trust

I once wrote a proposal to the owner of my employer. We desperately needed to increase the amount of leave each employee could accrue each pay period. I provided him factual reasons and financially justified each. Even though he did not institute a new policy right away, I planted a seed. Cultural and methodological changes do not happen overnight.

A couple of years ago, I knew that a client was scaling back a task order due to budget restraints. I was going to have to let three of seven people go just before the holidays. Since there was available funding on the task, I pleaded with the client to grant a no cost extension (a common practice in my industry), but to no avail. He said his hands were tied.

I kept in touch with the team members and told them as much as I could. Behind the scenes, I was also recommending to my chain-of-command that they find other positions in the company for these individuals. I did everything I could. Although I wasn't able to change the outcome, I earned the respect of my client, my team members, and my chain-of-command.

44. Place the right candidate in the right position

When you are a manager, promote your employees based on their individual strengths, not a title.

An individual with a sour personality would not be the ideal employee to greet customers at the front desk. A vivacious employee would not be suited to a mundane job either. It is highly important to place employees in positions in which they thrive. Otherwise, they probably will leave the company.

Get to know your employees. Discover their interests and their skillset. Marry these with your vacancies and you have a strong team.

An employee's technical expertise may propel him quickly up the ladder. More accolades, higher salary. However, in order for his company to remain profitable, and perhaps bid him competitively on contracts, they may have to promote him and give him additional responsibilities. Bad move. Just because he is a technical expert does not mean he should become a manager and lead people. He may not have the requisite people skills.

This trend is changing in some larger companies. They are acknowledging that there are two types of leaders, and they offer two distinct paths for advancement: one for management personnel, and one for technical personnel. They reward the fruits of everyone's labor while recognizing that all are not equal.

45. Don't be defined by titles

Is it possible to be a certified Project Manager, but not be an effective leader? You bet. Just as a teacher might have a license, but he is not a good teacher.

An effective leader does not need the title. They need a "take charge" spirit who delegates effectively, is flexible, and motivates their employees.

46. Adapt

Like the U.S. Coast Guard's motto, "Semper Paratus" ("Always Ready"), a good leader is always vigilant and tackles whatever comes their way. They can adapt to changes independently without being instructed to do so.

Take notice of our greatest leaders in history and follow their role. Adapt quickly to situations and overcome adversities with resolve.

Do what is right, not what is easy.

— Susie Orman

&❧

47. Do not overpay/underpay employees

Just as you would not want to be shortchanged, ensure your employees' salaries are commensurate with their experience and positions.

Remain competitive with other companies. Do not risk losing a talented employee to another company in a year.

Consequently, you don't want to overpay an employee and not be able to fund another position. Football teams experience this every year with contract negotiations and free agency.

48. Delegate

If you are a leader, it is not physically possible for you to work "in the weeds" all the time.

Get to know each employee's strengths and weaknesses. Know who you can delegate tasks to without missing a beat. This will free you to focus on more high-level tasks. If you do not delegate, chances are you will bottleneck progress.

Do not micromanage. This causes your subordinates to feel incompetent and unappreciated.

49. Take Risks

Lucky people are lucky because they first take risks. You cannot hang onto the shore and expect to explore the ocean. Likewise, you cannot experience the thrill of an icy mountain if you stay on the bunny slope. Embrace every opportunity that presents itself.

Apply the glass-half-full approach and view a perceived threat as a challenge. What is the worse that could happen? You will still be the same person if you fail at a challenge, but you will learn and grow in the process.

The tasks you ignore are the ones you fear.
                    — Adam Braun, *Pencils of Promise*

&❧

50. Under-promise, over-deliver

Expectations can get you into trouble if you do not set realistic ones upfront.

When I helped manage the service department for a yacht broker, I learned very quickly that maintaining a boat was far different than servicing a car. Unlike a car dealership, where customers bring their cars to the shop, our service staff had to travel to various marinas throughout the region. Without a software system to integrate travel time, time to repair, a general schedule, and other variables like the weather, I frequently found myself being chewed out by angry customers.

I learned to shift their expectations upfront by explaining all the variables that could push the due date to the right. This forced them to keep their personal schedules more fluid, and they were more understanding of schedule changes.

51. Create a fun environment

In the book, *FISH! – A Remarkable Way to Boost Morale and Improve Results*, co-authored by Stephen C. Lundin, Harry Paul, and John Christensen, an employee is assigned to manage a failing division. Her subordinates were rude, morale was low, and customers were irate at the service (or lack thereof) that they had received.

After several weeks, down-hearted and depressed, the manager passed by the fishmongers at Pikes Place Fish Market in Seattle. She was drawn like a magnet to their camaraderie and enthusiasm. They were comedians in an interactive play, puppeteering dead fish, giving them accents, and tossing them around. Onlookers enthusiastically cheered at their antics.

This inspires the manager. She establishes a plan to clean up the negative environment of her office. She takes her team to the fish market, and they brainstorm ways they can make their work enjoyable. It was just a matter of time before they did just that!

You will be surprised how powerful you can be when you infect others with your enthusiasm.
— Kitty Holding

&

Devise ways you can build each other up. Here are just a few ideas you may employ:

- Periodic lunches out of the office
- Happy hours
- Establish a football pool
- Bring donuts or bagels once a month
- Gather together a power walker team
- Incentivize employees based on what drives them

In a typical work week, you may see your fellow employees more hours than you do your own family. Make it enjoyable for them and they will make it enjoyable for you. Perfect your own imperfect job.

52. Keep up with technology

In the 1980's, archaic DOS-based computer programs displayed green block-styled letters and numbers on a curved black monitor.

Then, as 1990 approached, Microsoft built its empire, developing personal databases, and personal website management. GUI (Graphical User Interface) with pictures and arrows buried DOS and it's horrendous scripts once and for all.

Almost as soon as it boomed, the internet ".com" businesses crashed. Things eventually stabilized, and today, the internet has remained the backbone of business and the economy. Desktop computers have become faster and smaller. Bulky laptops, car telephones, cameras, boom-boxes, and encyclopedias have become practically obsolete with the birth of the smart phone. What's next is anyone's guess.

What are you doing to learn, grow, and keep up with the advances in technology? As you climb the ladder, don't become a technological dinosaur. Learn continuously. Take classes. Stay on top of your game.

Practice success before you are successful.
— Dan Pena

ॐ

53. Teleworking/Telecommuting

What is the difference between telecommuting and teleworking?

Telecommuting is working from a remote location once or twice a week. *Tele-working* is working from a remote location for an extended period of time. Both are convenient if you have children, an aging parent, or if you or a family member has an illness that requires periodic doctor visits. It is also helpful if you relocate with your spouse's job and you want to see if it works out first before you quit your career.

If you wish to telework or telecommute, ask. Draft a proposal. Make it a win-win situation for you and your company.

Also note that if you are not physically in the office, make yourself invisibly visible to your co-workers and managers. Have a good cable connection, otherwise you will be under constant stress.

Speaking from experience, Teleworking is isolating and you may feel as though you are under house arrest. Your co-workers, who work various hours during a day, may take advantage your status as an off-site employee. Your 8-hr day could quickly turn into a 12-hour day if you allow it. Do not feel pressured to be on duty during all hours. Set your boundaries. Otherwise, you could quickly come to neglect the very people you are telecommuting for in the first place – your family.

Force yourself to get out every once in a while to try and find friends who could relate to your work status. Attend Chamber of Commerce meetings in the area. Make sure you find camaraderie, positive reinforcement, and companionship.

Be honest. Record actual time worked on your timecard. Never cheat.

Understand that this situation may hinder your upward mobility within your company.

Managers, I advise you to think twice before approving proposals to allow employees to telecommute or telework. Make sure they have valid reasons. If they are the right employees for your company, they should make work a priority, not an afterthought. However, be flexible enough with your employees so that they are able to maintain a good life balance. Allow them to make up their hours later if they want to see their daughter's elementary school graduation, take an elderly parent to the grocery store, or nurse a sick spouse back to health. Refrain from approving long-term telecommuting or teleworking proposals because it isn't good for your employees, whether they know it or not. Plus it injects a certain degree of risk into your project.

Ensure you are getting quality from your personnel who telework, telecommute, or work revised schedules so that they have a regular day off. Frequently touch base with them and invite them to participate in meetings via conference calls.

54. Clearly define roles and responsibilities

Everyone in a company needs to know the game plan and rule book, whether you are on a football field or in a factory. Without a plan, chaos erupts. This is even more important as your company grows.

In small businesses especially, employees wear many hats. Each of these hats must be defined, so that all are clear on what they are supposed to do, how each job interrelates, and management expectations. Once these roles and responsibilities are determined, they must be documented.

Ensure each department develops and shares:
1. An organizational chart.
2. Clearly defined roles and responsibilities.
3. Formal flowcharts to depict daily operations.

Once documented remember to maintain them and keep them up-to-date.

Create a clear vision for you and your team. Know the goal and be able to present it clearly to the team, allowing them to share in your vision. Then together, take the steps necessary to accomplish it.

Vision without action is merely a dream. Action without vision just passes the time. Vision with action can change the world.

— Joel Barker

&

55. Create a fluid business plan and mission statement

Many things can affect your business daily, even something as simple as the weather. Imagine how companies in NYC were affected the weeks following 9/11. As much as a successful person must be agile, so too should a company. Markets are forever changing; competition changes; employees leave the company. Do not let the ink dry on your business and project plans. Review and update them periodically. Share your business plan with your management team, otherwise, how will they know your expectations for your company?

Likewise, share your mission statement with the entire company. You will have fewer disgruntled employees if you make it known and clear upfront.

Ponder the yellowed mission statement hanging in the cheap frame at your entranceway, placed there by your secretary five years ago. Does any of it still apply? Chances are you've obtained new clients, new employees, and new cultural changes. Have you ventured off course from what you originally intended? As a company CEO or COO, you may have reached an impasse. Should you charge on or change your mission statement?

Be able to recognize when change is happening and take the necessary steps to adapt your company to it. It is the evolution of business. As the adage goes, "the only thing in life that is constant is change."

No one exceeds beyond their wildest expectations unless they have them to begin with.
— Ralph Clowell

৪৬

56. Limit communication

What?! Limit communication? Yes, hear me out.

With our electronic tethers, employees receive correspondence late into the evening. This causes stress. Unnecessary stress.

To alleviate this burden on your employees, build a structured communications plan. Schedule a morning or afternoon meeting daily or weekly, depending on the need for everyone to share ideas and status.

Another approach is to require subordinates provide a status report at the end of each day. This eliminates all of the little, bothersome messages throughout the day.

Additionally, set a rule that requires all correspondence be held during normal business hours only unless of a dire emergency. (Make sure you define a "dire emergency.")

57. Avoid getting tangled in red-tape

While the devil is often in the details, good leaders know how to delegate trivial matters to their subordinates. They do not micromanage.

Make known your expectations, and keep the lines of communication open. Even though I suggest not getting into the weeds, owners and senior leadership can become too separated from their employees if they are not careful. In large companies, it's relatively easy to get stove-piped in an area of expertise or niche. Never stop learning and reaching out to your subordinates.

58. Honor loyal clients

Key customers are customers who always return to your company to buy a product or service. This loyalty can be one of your greatest marketing assets. Positive, word-of-mouth advertising is invaluable.

Find ways to honor these customers. Call them periodically. Are they satisfied with their purchase? What about the service they received? What else can you do for them?

Think of clever, inexpensive ways to garner their continued support and expand your business within the community. Send them a gift certificate, a holiday card, or VIP access to an open house. Give them a referral bonus. Regardless of the mechanism, take time to foster this crucial relationship.

No one cares how much you know, until they know how much you care.
— **Theodore Roosevelt**

&

59. Satisfy the golden triangle

Customers, employees and stockholders make up what I commonly refer to as the "golden triangle." It is difficult to please all three simultaneously, even though each is equally important.

At the core of this triangle is — you guessed it — money. Salaries must be high enough to entice employees, fair enough to the customer, and low enough to assume a profit that would benefit the stockholders. Imagine the difficulty! Once a company becomes publicly traded, a manager not only has to worry about his employees and customers, but now the company's stockholders. His company's website has to contain all the buzz-words; they vie to be ranked by various magazines, state organizations and other important-sounding groups. All of these are necessary, along with good numbers, to keep their stock valued high.

This truly is a numbers game, based on knowledge of the business, math skills, and a little bit of luck. The most successful CEO's are highly experienced at keeping the balance.

60. Know what motivates others

Everyone has a different motivating factor. Something that propels them out of bed each morning. Something that keeps them at your company instead of moving to another one.

I know of five main motivating factors:

- Flexibility/Time off
- Title/Prestige
- Stability/Security
- Praise/Respect
- Money/Benefits

Know what motivates each one of your team members. Always seek to balance their needs with the goals of the company.

If your actions inspire others to dream more, learn more, do more and become more, you are a leader.

— John Quincy Adams

෫

61. Uplift others

The golden rule is to "do unto others as you would have them do unto you."

Make a list of all the bosses you ever had. Place their names into two columns: "Bad bosses" and "Good bosses." I'm 100% certain that all of those good bosses had a common characteristic: they uplifted others by praising them, allowing flexibility, appreciating their work, and so-forth.

This is a very simple exercise in knowing what it takes to be a good leader/boss. Learn from those who have gone before you.

62. Practice formal Project Management

The core of formal project management is taking a project and breaking it down into its main tasks and subtasks, assigning priorities and due dates. All of these actions are required to achieve the goal – completion of the project, and full satisfaction of your customer.

Good project management skills can be practiced in every aspect of life. For example, let's say you want to be a rock star. First, you have to know how to play an instrument or sing. (However these days, after watching the multitude of talent contests on television, one does not seem to have to even carry a tune!)

The project first needs to be defined. At what level of stardom do you wish to achieve? Do you want to open for Aerosmith, or do you want to BE Aerosmith?

Once you note the end goal, list the main components and subcomponents of the ladder to stardom. Here is an example I presented to my musician husband at the onset of his career:

- Get Gigs
    - Make a list of venues to visit
    - Hand out demo's
        - Develop demo
    - Hand out literature
        - Make business cards
            - Have pictures taken
        - Create flyers
    - Create a contract template
- Develop a Fan Base
    - Create a Facebook account
    - Create a website with show schedule
    - Sell promotional items
        - Make coozies
- Publish first solo CD
    - Write music
    - Create budget
    - Decide on a recording studio
        - Interview Studio 1
        - Interview Studio 2

It may seem like a lot of work, but each intricate piece of the puzzle has to fit. This is called a Work Breakdown Structure (WBS).

Assign due dates, and what resources can accomplish each. Perhaps your cousin works at a restaurant that hires live musicians. You can even add in the cost for each to find out how much cash you'll need for your venture into stardom.

Organize, don't agonize.

- Nancy Pelosi

୫७

63. Institute periodic performance reviews

Survey your employees often. Process them, analyze them, and provide thoughtful feedback. Always be open to change and recommendations from your employees. You are not always right.

Appraisals that incorporate both chain-of-command and peer evaluations are ideal. Let's face it, everyone has a different opinion. Also, the boss cannot be everywhere at one time.

Individual Development Plans are necessary to help foster employee growth and longevity. However, the goal is not to come up with as many synonyms for "great" as possible. It isn't to hone your creative writing skills. Quite simply, an appraisal should list an employee's accomplishments and pitfalls. It is an honest assessment of an employee's work efforts and work ethic. Don't make it a personality contest. Just because you are Joe's brother's cousin does not make him a better employee than Sally.

In order to provide a true assessment, set objectives early on. Established objectives should be measurable. Not implied, but explicit, written goals for the specified time period (I recommend 6 months to 1 year). If you tie raises and promotions to reviews, ensure you have a scale and make this scale available to all employees. Don't leave them in the dark, guessing as to why Joe got more of a raise than Sally. People talk.

64. Budget wisely

Managers must work from a budget. If you don't have a budget, you will quickly overspend. The larger the company, the larger your budget. Gather teams to help review it. Are you spending too much on fancy pens when that money might be better served on spot bonuses and gift cards for your employees? Put people before money. Give them a sense of meaning and purpose.

An effective manager ensures a project is not only delivered on-budget, but on-time and at the quality expected. Often a manager's focus is on schedule and cost. Quality is lost along the way, as more output is expected.

Don't tell me what you value, show me your budget, and I'll tell you what you value.

- Joe Biden

&❧

65. Fail together

In past wars, great generals and commanders often led their soldiers into battle. Being at the frontlines was a symbol of strength and bravery. It gave their soldiers confidence to take on the enemy.

Similarly, your subordinates look to you to lead. Successful teams share a mutual give and take. Take one for the team if necessary.

Find success through failure.

– Michael Jordan

&❧

66. Institute the right business model

Flat organizations consist of one leader (usually the owner and a couple of his counterparts) overseeing the rest of the company. In my experience, this organizational model does not work as a company expands. There needs to be levels of management in order to keep the lines of communication open with every employee.

Although the concept of a flat organization seeks to save money by eliminating layers of "frosting," it is this "frosting" that binds together the cake (aka, company). Let's face it, people are needy. It is human nature. Your employees are no exception. You need middle managers, and perhaps several layers of middle management depending on the size of your company.

67. Control growth

Ensure your company builds a solid infrastructure to support growth. Infrastructure consists of the accounting, human resources, and IT departments. They are the cornerstone of the business.

I've seen it happen more than once. A company starts out small and then it grows too fast. They win a new contract and staff it without giving thought to the infrastructure. The existing accounting department, for example, may not be able to keep up with the increasing demands of the new employees. They have to set them up in the accounting system, process their travel claims, timecards, etc.

The accounting team members burn out. Corporate ignores their complaints. One-by-one, they leave the company. New accountants replace them and make mistakes, costing the company thousands of dollars. It is detrimental. The downward spiral has begun.

This illustration proves that Infrastructure needs to be built accordingly. Otherwise the business will falter in either production or quality. Even during the most strenuous growth periods, the bones of the company should never be left to chance.

Conversely, downsize if you need to. Do not delay. Find the proper ratio of infrastructure to personnel for your company and do not delineate from it.

68. Cross-train employees

Employees do not like to be stagnant. They enjoy learning and growing. Give them opportunities to cross-train and compete with one another. A team in a dynamic atmosphere will thrive.

Cross-training benefits the company as well. It enables team members to have back-up when they take vacation.

69. Don't try to please everyone

At times, you may be pulled by corporate staff and clients simultaneously, oftentimes in different directions. Both tug your time. Both are important. How do you cope?

It is a seemingly impossible task to keep everyone happy all the time. However, as mentioned previously, if you remain organized and communicative, you can manage effectively. The last thing you want to do is make enemies, but you also cannot make everyone happy. Instead, know your allies, and lean on them in times of trouble.

70. Stay competitive

To compete in today's market, you cannot allow yourself to get outsourced or automated. As companies, we cannot be the "generals" of the 60's and 70's (General Motors, General Electric, General Mills, etc.), all part of a diminishing good-ole boys network.

We also cannot preach customer service, total quality management or even Six Sigma. We even have to look beyond the recent trends of social media.

In today's fast-paced, demanding life, it is all about "the experience." How do we do this? Hire fresh employees each year to gain a new perspective into your future customers. Consumer expectations become exponentially higher each year.

As a business, we must determine what new, amazing thing is on the horizon. As a team, we must think about how our business fits with this new concept, methodology, or product. We must ensure our entire team, from the administrative personnel to the executive staff knows their role in the big scheme.

71. Take your vacation time

Making memories with your family far outweighs any project on the job. Getting away refreshes the psyche.
It boggles my mind that managers leave personal time on the books each year! It seems as though the more senior you are in an organization, the more personal time off you get, but the less you use.

Senior management never seem to unplug. They answer emails even when they should be at Disney World, enjoying their families.

You must learn to trust your subordinates. No man is an island. Establish a guidebook with instructions, similarly to what teachers leave for substitutes. All organizations need to cross-train their employees. It not only keeps them engaged, but benefits the company by having backup of its resources.

Whoever is careless with the truth in small matters cannot be trusted with important matters.

- Albert Einstein

ℰ❥

72. Maintain a strong life balance

Something that has not changed in my lifetime is the 8-hour work day. It is hard to believe that before Labor unions of the early 20th century rescued us, we were working 12-hour days.

With today's technology, we can do so much with less, but we are expected to produce more within the same timeframe. People are already stretched thin. As a manager, do not expect longer than an 8-hour day from your employees. Everyone deserves a life outside of work.

At the end of your work day, leave work as soon as you get into your car to go home. Listen to the radio to decompress from the grueling workday. Once you get home, focus solely on your family and hobbies. Take it from me, this will save precious relationships and your overall sanity.

Here are some ways to reduce stress:

-Get Organized
- Clean your workspace
- Make a "To Do" List and prioritize it

-Decompress
- Turn off email and cell phone, radio

-Take frequent breaks throughout the day

-Meet your physical needs
- Eat, sleep, exercise

-Make the most of free time
- Date your significant other
- Play with your children
- Visit aging parents

-Work to live, don't live to work
- If you want to start a family, do so
- Don't miss the concert or the graduation
- You can't get those moments back...

Steven Covey, in *Seven Habits of Highly Effective People,* advises to "put first things first." This is necessary to achieve the life you desire.

To keep the body in good health is a duty. Otherwise we should not be able to keep our mind strong and clear.

-Buddha

೮෴

73. Put your Family First

All women must decide whether to return to work after the birth of a child. This is your choice. You don't need to do what your mother did. You don't need to do what your best friend does. This is a personal choice. Whether you decide to homeschool or return to your corporate office, you are caring for your family. Never allow yourself to feel guilt.

Find daycare you trust. This is the most important decision for the working parent. I must have interviewed fifty in-home daycare providers before I found the perfect one for our family.

Perhaps you want the best of both worlds. I switched to part-time status to care for my nursing infant. As long as I performed my work to the best of my ability, my teammates did not discriminate against me.

You may even come up with a creative job strategy to accommodate your family. As a Gen-X businesswoman, I was the first at my company to telecommute. We were moving with my husband's job and I knew I would not find a job in that area. Luckily my client loved my work. I put together a proposal that was vetted and accepted by both my company and client.

Please understand that the journey of life is not a straight line. The detours are what makes it fun, challenging, and worth living. Do what you feel is best at every turn. Remember that whatever you do, you are always a role model for your children.

Never apologize for putting family first. You will never regret doing so.

Family is not an important thing. It's everything.
-Michael J. Fox

&♥

REACHING THE PROFESSIONAL LEVEL

PASSING THE BATON

Once I remarried, I returned to the job market. The reason being, my husband was a musician and our paths crossed only briefly every afternoon. I was just getting home when he was leaving for a gig! This was frustrating!

Since he could not play gigs in the early morning, I decided to quit management and get a part time job in an entirely different industry (yachting). Working part-time enabled me to see more of my husband. It was also eye-opening for someone who essentially had never left government contracting. Here, I gained an entirely new title - Service Writer.

I began to mentor others and decided I no longer wished to climb the ladder. I learned that it was time to pass the baton to the up-and-coming generation. To a life-long, goal-minded go-getter, this was a milestone. However, it felt good. It was time.

Two years later, I revaluated my life and switched jobs again. At this point, all I wanted a stable job, stable income, and little to no stress. My journey was moving me into yet another direction. I had hit my middle years and my priorities had changed.

৪৬

Stacey R. James

74. Pay it forward

No one likes to be stagnant. In some small companies, there is not a lot of room for growth. Take the opportunity as someone's manager to improve their career. Provide constructive criticism and give them advice. Work the puzzle together, fitting in any pieces they may be missing. Remember your own mentors and how they helped you grow.

75. Don't let age hinder you

The cover of a fashion magazine in the grocery store check-out line announces, "50 is the new 30!"

Age is becoming less and less of a barrier to getting what you want out of life. We are healthier and are living longer. View this as an opportunity, not a hindrance.

My divorce lawyer became a lawyer in her fifties. Somewhere I read that an 80-year-old woman became an archeologist.

Stephen M. Pollen writes in his book, *Second Acts*:
- Examine the internal and external barriers and chip away at them.
- If money is the issue, cut expenses and find creative ways to earn/borrow money.
- Unlock your vision for your future – daydream!

Enrich your life. You do not necessarily need schooling to do so. Become a self-proclaimed doctorate in an area of interest. Suppose you like 16th century art. Study it. Visit museums. Read about the artists and visit their hometowns. Learn about the chemistry of the paints used, and how the paints were made. Study the culture to gain a deeper meaning behind your favorite.

You never need to "put yourself out to pasture" and you are never really "Over-the-hill." Stay interested and stay interesting!

Once you make a decision, the universe conspires to make it happen.
— Ralph Waldo Emerson
&

76. Reassess yourself and know when to move on

You're on an airplane, sitting on the tarmac, rain pouring all around from the dark gray sky. The captain has warned passengers that it will be a bumpy ride because of a cold front.

The plane zooms down the runway, lifts off the ground and proceeds through the fog and downpour. It hits air pockets, causing you to feel you are on an ascending rollercoaster losing its grip on the tracks.

You cannot see out of the window, and you can only hope and pray you will make it out alive. All of a sudden, the plane ascends from the depths of darkness into a sunny world. You look down on the thick blanket of white clouds from whence you emerged.

Isn't this life? Don't we often get caught up in the dark situations that we are not able to see the situation for what it is? What if we lift ourselves beyond our clouds and open our hearts to light and life? You have but one life to live. What would you do if you knew you only had a short time remaining on this earth? What is causing hindering you in following your dreams?

Continue to learn and remain proactive. Take time to reevaluate where you spend your 40+ hours every week. Are you suffering from burnout? Do you need a vacation? A leave of absence? Or a permanent change of jobs? If you feel you can't take it anymore, ask to switch departments, or find a temporary job elsewhere.

Based on first-hand experience, a change can be refreshing. Life is too short to feel miserable day in and day out. It's okay to say "no" in every aspect of life. This is *your* life, not anyone else's.

Have a backup plan. Prepare. My ex-father-in-law ingrained in me the adage, "Proper preparation prevents poor performance!"

Everyone has a conscious, gut, or sixth-sense. Whatever you wish to call it, listen to it. It can guide you through this life and enable you to live the life you wish to live.

Everyone around you may say you are lucky. That because your company offers frequent happy hours, an on-site gym, and free Starbucks-quality coffee you are so fortunate. However, in your heart, you feel stifled.

You are not growing. You have become pigeon-holed. Simply put, you are not happy.

By now you should know that there are plenty of other fish in the sea. America is still bustling with opportunity! All you need to do is seek out your next one.

Don't look back on your life one day and have regrets. Clothe yourself with the right attitude. A better job or career could be around the bend.

Simply possessing a talent or skill isn't enough. To gain satisfaction from that strength, use it in a way that is meaningful to you.

— **Unknown**

෨

77. Establish a Life Resume

A life resume is not a resume or profile as described earlier. Instead, this is a document for you and only you. It is a tool you can use to see where you've been, what you've accomplished, and what you hope to accomplish in the future. There is no set format. Be creative.

What has gotten you to where you are today? Are you happy? If you were not afraid of failure, what would you do? Do you wish to go through life working at a dead-end job?

If you are an outdoor person, why are you behind a computer in a cubicle performing data entry? If you prefer to manage a workforce vice addressing adolescent attitudes, why do you remain a teacher?

I update my life resume frequently and meditate on my career. I use it when I'm feeling down or depressed. (This very book is part of my life resume!)

Just as you obtain car or home insurance policies, you need a career insurance policy. You do not get this from your employer, because no employer guarantees your job for infinity. Nor can you guarantee life roadblocks that may cause you to need to change directions: divorce, death, marriage, etc.

I fully believe that happiness on this earth is wholly knowing who you are, what you like, and focusing on that. It is not envying others. It is not running yourself ragged by trying to keep-up-with-the-Joneses.

Become your dream.
— Adam Braun, *Pencils of Promise*
෮

78. Build a profile, not a resume
It is a competitive world. Should you decide on a career change, there is no need to regurgitate every job and accomplishment on a resume. Rather, create a profile, and make it eye-catching.

Include a professional photograph, especially if you will be a front desk receptionist or someone who comes into contact frequently with your customers. Once, to put a picture of yourself on a resume was faux pas, but this is the age of social media! A recruiter is going to look at your profile on LinkedIn.com anyway. Save them a step. Get ahead of the other candidates.

Choose a font and set-up that reveals your style. Chronological is no longer the norm. Highlight the most important areas of your experience and don't forget to cater each bullet point to the desired position. Make sure your qualifications fit the person the employer is seeking.

It may be that those who do most dream most.
— Stephen Leacoch

දෙ

79. Give Back to Your Community

Look for opportunities to serve others. Volunteer your time doing something aligned with your job or a hobby you enjoy.

For example, if you are a web designer and your child's 5th grade graduation needs a brochure. Volunteer to make it.
Suppose a neighboring family has been in a horrible car accident and needs money. You happen to have been involved with fundraisers in the past and know some philanthropists. Contact them.

The sky's the limit! Serving others isn't a chore. By giving of your time, money and expertise to others, you are getting back triple-fold, and setting a positive example for future generations.

Make little decisions with head, big decisions with heart.

—Adam Braun, *Pencils of Promise*

ℰ

80. Save for a rainy day

You don't need the iced mocha *every* day.

Treat yourself occasionally, and know that if you were to fall on tough times, you'd have a comfortable cushion to fall upon. A rule of thumb is to have 6-month's salary in the bank.

Never live beyond your means. Just because you make a certain amount of money does not mean you need to spend it. Most millionaires became that way because they simply saved.

My father had a stroke in his early 40's. Lucky for us, he saved a large portion of his salary. We were not impacted financially as we would have been had he insisted on fancy houses, cars, etc.

A man is not old until regrets take the place of dreams.

— John Barrymore

ℰ

Stacey R. James

EPILOGUE

Well there you have it! Three sections of my life, with 80 lessons I've learned thus far in my career!

God-willing, I have many more years ahead of me. The next chapter of my life will most likely cover slowing down, retiring, long term care, and grandchildren. I often refer to this next book as, "Chapter 4."

I no longer define myself by what I do. I no longer define success by how well I have performed in a job. Instead, I am me, and my most successful accomplishment has been raising a daughter to be inquisitive, self-reliant, down to earth, self-assured and resilient. She is remarkable, and I hope she passes along all of these lessons -as well as those of her own - to future generations.

Now, as she plans for college, Hubby and I prepare to head west...

Roads? Where we going we don't need roads!
    - Dr. Emmett Brown, *Back to the Future.*

ॐ

The End

Stacey R. James

ABOUT THE AUTHOR

Stacey R. James has written numerous technical publications throughout her professional career, but *Successful Leadership Principles,* is her light-hearted, concise guide to succeeding in the business world. She imparts nuggets of wisdom to every reader - whether a recent graduate or a mid-life career-changer.

With a quick wit and a hefty bit of common sense, she tells her own story of how a simple job morphed into a flourishing career and happy life. Stacey's mission is to help others by sharing her own experiences.

Stacey lives with her family in Baltimore, Maryland.

She would love to hear from her fans. Please contact her at **staceyrjames@yahoo.com**.